SandCastle 1

What Color is it?

Orange

Mary Elizabeth Salzmann

ABDO
Publishing Company

Published by SandCastle™, an imprint of ABDO Publishing Company, 4940 Viking Drive, Edina, Minnesota 55435.

Printed in the United States.

Cover and Interior Photo credits: Adobe, Díamar, Digital Stock, John Foxx, PhotoDisc

Library of Congress Cataloging-in-Publication Data

Salzmann, Mary Elizabeth, 1968–
        Orange / Mary Elizabeth Salzmann.
            p.   cm. -- (What color is it?)
        Summary: Simple text and photographs present a variety of orange
things, including a pumpkin, ball, and life jacket.
        ISBN 1-57765-158-8
        1. Colors--Juvenile literature. 2. Orange (Color)--Juvenile
literature. [1. Orange (Color). 2. Color.] I. Title.
        II. Series: Salzmann, Mary Elizabeth, 1968–   What color is it?
        QC495.5.S27   1999
        535.6--dc21   98-26681
                                                                                CIP
                                                                                AC   r98

The SandCastle concept, content, and reading method have been reviewed and approved by a national advisory board including literacy specialists, librarians, elementary school teachers, early childhood education professionals, and parents.

Let Us Know

After reading the book, SandCastle would like you to tell us your stories about reading. What is your favorite page? Was there something hard that you needed help with? Share the ups and downs of learning to read. We want to hear from you! To get posted on the Abdo Publishing Company Web site, send us email at:

sandcastle@abdopub.com

About SandCastle™

Nonfiction books for the beginning reader

- Basic concepts of phonics are incorporated with integrated language methods of reading instruction. Most words are short, and phrases, letter sounds, and word sounds are repeated.

- Readability is determined by the number of words in each sentence, the number of characters in each word, and word lists based on curriculum frameworks.

- Full-color photography reinforces word meanings and concepts.

- "Words I Can Read" list at the end of each book teaches basic elements of grammar, helps the reader recognize the words in the text, and builds vocabulary.

- Reading levels are indicated by the number of flags on the castle.

Look for more SandCastle books in these three reading levels:

Level 1 (one flag)	Level 2 (two flags)	Level 3 (three flags)
Grades Pre-K to K 5 or fewer words per page	**Grades K to 1** 5 to 10 words per page	**Grades 1 to 2** 10 to 15 words per page

This starfish
is orange.

My pumpkin
is orange.

My hat is orange.

My phone
is orange.

My ball is orange.

My shirt is orange.

My life vest
is orange.

My hair is orange.

My hair is
orange, too.

Words I Can Read

Nouns

A **noun** is a person, place, or thing

ball (BAWL), p. 13

hair (HAIR), pp. 19, 21

hat (HAT), p. 9

life vest (LIFE VEST), p. 17

phone (FONE), p. 11

pumpkin (PUHMP-kin), p. 7

shirt (SHURT), p. 15

starfish (STAR-fish), p. 5

Verbs

A **verb** is an action or being word

is (IZ), pp. 5, 7, 9, 11, 13, 15, 17, 19, 21

Sight Words

ball

phone

hair

pumpkin

hat

shirt

life vest

starfish